FUNNY ENGLISH

Learn ENGLISH Naturally With the Aid of JOKES

Table of Contents

How to make use of this book 8

Doctors and patients 10

Police 15

Family 19

Teachers and students 25

Husband and wife 29

Old people 36

Animals 41

Stupid people 45

Miscellaneous 50

How to make use of this book

Learning another language can be dull and boring oftentimes. Nouns, adjectives, tenses and grammar are all challenging and easy to forget unless they are dealt with practically and naturally. Students try to write, read, do courses and so on, but always they find themselves hopeless and making mistakes.

So how to overcome these difficulties?

How to develop our second language?

The answer is very simple:

LEARN THE LANGUAGE IN ITS NATURAL CONTEXT.

In fact the most effective method of mastering any language is to get involved in real practice of the language rather than memorizing and doing tests. Thus, why do not we change our attitude and learn naturally?

All the tools and materials are available starting with videos and ending with travel and reading. And the most effective type of reading is the one that makes you more interested and entertained.

Nothing like jokes can interest and amuse us. They create an enjoyable atmosphere and put a smile on our faces. And above all, they stick in our memory forever because **our memories save data which is related to some feelings or emotions.** (for example, when we are shocked by some news we will remember this news for years — when we go on an exciting vacation with our loved ones, we will remember all of the details for years ...). Jokes usually make us overjoyed and happy every time we hear or tell them. They can stick in memory without any effort, giving us a great deal of grammar, nouns, verbs, adjectives, idioms in a way that makes them present in our mind and ready to use. For this reason, I truly recommend jokes as a natural method of learning the language in a funny and interesting manner.

Read the joke, laugh at it, post it on social media networks, share it with friends and tell it to others. Congratulations !!! You have mastered it.

This is a perfect way of practice in which you will not only develop your conversation skills but also learn grammar, words and the like naturally. You are going to be amazed at how fast you will improve.

Unfortunately, some believe that incorporating humor and fun in the learning process can be distracting and unprofessional.

But recent research has found that injecting enjoyable activities into the learning process helps foster long-term memory. Adrenaline, dopamine, and endorphins are released when our bodies respond to positive and heartening moments. When this happens during a lesson or while listening to or reading a joke, it allows us to absorb the topic being taught or read more effectively.

Another reason is that the integration of entertainment helps all of adults, teens and the little ones stay more relaxed, reducing the tension they feel. If they are in this comfortable state, then they can engage and learn better and faster. Smile and laughter improve our moods, make us chill out and take it easy. This can be achieved with the help of funny jokes. In addition, by evoking an enjoyable atmosphere, learners become more interested and motivated to get more and more information.

Let us take this joke as an example and see how can we make use of it:

Little Johnny asks the teacher, "Mrs. Roberts, can I be <u>punished for</u> something I haven't done?"

Mrs. Roberts is <u>shocked</u>, "Of course not, Johnny, that would be very <u>unfair!</u>"

Little Johnny is <u>relieved</u>, "OK Mrs. Roberts, sorry, <u>I haven't done my homework.</u>"

What can we learn from this joke?

Well, first of all, it makes sense to spend some time smiling or laughing at it. Then, let's find out what good words and grammar are there?

- **To be punished for (doing)** something. (a verb and its preposition).
- **Of course not.** (a very good way to say "No").
- **Unfair:** (an adjective that means not following the rules)
- **Relieved:** (an adjective that means to be happy that something unpleasant has not happened or has ended).

- "I haven't done my homework": (1. present perfect tense: used for telling results. 2. do homework: using "do" for activities and studies).

Notice that you are learning grammar and vocabulary in a natural way and in the right place. For example, all people may know the meaning of "relieved" but they find it difficult to use it in the right place because they learned it by translation or some other way. By learning words and grammar from a joke, you will have the ability to use them correctly as a result of being able to remember full sentences rather than individual words.

(**Repetition is the mother of skill**) when you start telling the jokes to other people or share it somewhere, you are actually doing a good job memorizing it and it will absolutely stick in your memory with the help of repetition. Let's assume that you were waiting for some test results and you were feeling worried, and after a while you get a message;" you got a top score". What's a good word to say? Of course "I feel relieved". You see? We took it from the joke when Johnny felt relieved after the good answer of his teacher.

Another important point is to tell yourself while you are learning "That's a good sentence, I will make it mine" .. "that's a new word. I will learn it and use it". This way, the information becomes not only active and present in your brain but easy to use without any confusion or mistakes.

Here is another joke:

A little boy visits his farmer grandpa and watches him *milk the cows.*
The next day one of the cows runs away and grandpa is *really upset about it.*

"Don't worry, Grandpa," says the boy <u>helpfully</u>, "she can't have gone very far with <u>an empty tank.</u>"

We should ask ourselves, what can I learn from this joke?

- **Milk the cows.** (a verb phrase)
- **Run away.** (a phrasal verb)
- **Hopefully.** (an adverb)
- **Can't have gone.** (making deductions)
- **An empty tank.** (a noun phrase)

You do not have to worry about the grammatical classifications and details. What really matters is getting as many as you can like the above language and as a result you are sure to use the grammar correctly without thinking or worrying about it. You can use any phrase you want for conversations, writing and so on.

I would like to remind you once more that we are learning full phrases, adjectives, adverbs and the like in their natural context rather than individually. This is a proven and reliable way to use the language effectively and effortlessly.

With jokes, you kill two birds with one stone. You have a good time and you also develop your English. Please, don't just focus on the joke itself or just read it and go. It is essential to take notes or underline what you need to learn so that you improve yourself. After all, these jokes were told by native speakers of English and they are a real opportunity to learn the language correctly.

Now, it is your turn to take over and do the practice on your own. But remember to follow the steps mentioned above.

DOCTORS AND PATIENTS

Joke .. 1

Patient: Oh doctor, I'm just so nervous. This is my first operation. - Doctor: Don't worry. Mine too.

Joke .. 2

Doctor: Hello, did you come to see me with an eye problem?
Patient: Wow, yes, how can you tell?
Doctor: Because you came in through the window instead of the door.

Joke .. 3

Patient: Doctor help me please, every time I drink a cup of coffee I get this intense stinging in my eye.
Doctor: I suggest you remove the spoon before drinking.

Joke .. 4

Doctor: "Well - Mrs. Smith, it would seem that you're pregnant."
Mrs. Smith: "Sweet Jesus, that's wonderful, I'm pregnant?!"
Doctor: "I only said that it seems so. Here's our weight loss brochure."

Joke .. 5

Doctor: "Can you describe the snake that bit you?"
Patient: "Yes. It looked like an angry rope. "

Joke .. 6

A nurse sees a guy wheeling himself frantically down the hall of the hospital so she stops him and asks what's wrong.
He says, "I'm due to have an operation but I heard a nurse say, 'It's a very simple operation, don't worry, I'm sure it will be all right.'"
The nurse says, "That's okay, she was just trying to comfort you. What's so frightening about that?"

The guy replies, "She was talking to the doctor!"

Joke .. 7

The nurse told the parents of a newly born child, "You have a cute baby."
The smiling husband said, "I bet you say that to all new parents."
"No," she replied, "just to those whose babies really are good-looking."
The husband again asked "So what do you say to the others?"
The nurse replied, "The baby looks just like you."

Joke .. 8

When I went to get my vaccinations the young nurse told me she was very nervous as it was her first time. I told her to give it her best shot.

Joke .. 9

I went to casualty yesterday and said to the doctor, "I've been stung by a wasp, have you got anything for it?"
She asked, "Whereabouts is it?"
I said, "I don't know, it could be miles away by now."

Joke .. 10

A man visits a doctor for routine check-up.
During check-up he asks the doctor, "Do you think I'll live a long and healthy life then?"
Doctor replies, "I doubt it somehow. Mercury is in Uranus right now."
The man, little annoyed, says, "I don't come in here for any of that astrology nonsense."
The doctor replied, "Neither do I. My rectal thermometer just broke."

Joke .. 11

A dentist had an old lady patient who was very hard to handle. As soon as she sat in the chair, she panicked and would clamp her mouth shut so firmly that he couldn't get it open to work on her teeth.

One afternoon, on about the third try to treat the old lady, the dentist figured out a way to get the job done. He excused himself from the old lady, went back to the reception desk and told his receptionist that as soon as he was ready to work on the old lady's teeth, she was to move up behind her and jab her in the rear with a long pin.

Well the receptionist did what she was told, and sure enough, the old lady opened her mouth to holler and that opening, maintained with a pry to keep it that way, got the job done.

Finally finishing with his work, the dentist said, "Well now, that wasn't so bad, was it?"

"Nope, not so bad," said the old lady. "But I'll tell you this, I never expected to feel the pain of a toothache way down in my ass."

Joke .. 12

What time do you go to the dentist?
At tooth-hurty.

Joke .. 13

A gorgeous young redhead goes into the doctor's office and said that her body hurt wherever she touched it.

'Impossible!' says the doctor. 'Show me.'

The redhead took her finger, pushed on her left shoulder and screamed, then she pushed her elbow and screamed even more. She pushed her knee and screamed; Likewise she pushed her ankle and screamed. Everywhere she touched made her scream. The doctor said, 'You're not really a redhead, are you? 'Well, no' she said, 'I'm actually a blonde.' 'I thought so,' the doctor said. 'Your finger is broken.'

Joke .. 14

During a visit to the mental asylum, a visitor asked the Director how do you determine whether or not a patient should be institutionalized. 'Well,' said the Director, 'we fill up a bathtub, then we offer a teaspoon, a teacup and a bucket to the patient and ask him or her to empty the bathtub.'

'Oh, I understand,' said the visitor. 'A normal person would use the bucket because it's bigger than the spoon or the teacup.'

'No.' said the Director, 'A normal person would pull the plug.

Joke .. 15

During his physical examination, a doctor asked a man about his physical activity level.

He described a typical day this way:

"Well, yesterday afternoon, I took a five hour walk about 7km through some pretty rough terrain.

I waded along the edge of a lake. I pushed my way through brambles.

I got sand in my shoes and my eyes.

I avoided standing on a snake. I climbed several rocky hills.

I took a few 'leaks' behind some big trees.

The mental stress of it all left me shattered.

At the end of it all I drank eight beers"

Inspired by the story, the doctor said, "You must be one hell of an outdoors man."

"No," he replied, "I'm just a shit golfer."

Joke .. 16

A psychiatrist was testing the mentality of a patient.

"Do you ever hear voices without being able to tell who is speaking or where the voices are coming from?" asked the psychiatrist.

"As a matter of fact, I do," said the patient.

"And when does this happen?" asked the psychiatrist.

"Oh," said the patient, "when I answer the telephone."

Joke .. 17

A man walks into his doctor's office and sits down in the waiting room. While he is waiting his turn to be seen, a casual acquaintance walks in and sits down next to him.
The newcomer asks "W w what are yyy you ddd doing here?"
The man replies, "I am waiting to see the doctor."
"W wwhy dd do yyy you wwant to sss see hhim?" The man replies,
"Well, if you must know, I have a prostate problem.
" A pp prostate ppp problem, wwhat's ttthat?"
"Well, if you must know. I pee like you talk."

Joke .. 18

A man with a worried look on his face ran into a clinic and asked the doctor if he knew a way to stop the hiccups.
Without any warning, the doctor slapped him in the face.
Amazed and angry, the young man demanded the doctor explain his unusual behavior.
"Well," said the doctor, "You don't have the hiccups now, do you?" "No," answered the young man, but my wife out in the car still does!"

Joke .. 19

This woman rushed to see her doctor, looking very much worried and all strung out. She rattles off:
"Doctor, take a look at me. When I woke up this morning, I looked at myself in the mirror and saw my hair all wiry and frazzled up, my skin was all wrinkled and pasty, my eyes were bloodshot and bugging out, and I had this corpse-like look on my face! What's WRONG with me, Doctor!?"
The doctor looks her over for a couple of minutes, then calmly says: "Well, I can tell you that there isn't nothing wrong with your eyesight...."

Joke .. 20

A doctor says to his patient, "I have bad news and worse news".
"Oh dear, what's the bad news?" asks the patient.
The doctor replies, "You only have 24 hours to live."
"That's terrible", said the patient. "How can the news possibly be worse?"
The doctor replies, "I've been trying to contact you since yesterday."

Joke .. 21

Doctor: "I am not exactly sure of the cause. I think it could be due to alcohol."
Patient: "That's ok. I will come back when you are sober."

POLICE JOKES

Joke .. 1

Three men are riding on just one motorcycle. They pass a police patrol. The policeman shouts after them:
"Police! Stop your vehicle now!"
But they just continue driving past. The last man turns around and yells: „Sorry dude! We can't take you on, we're already one too many!"

Joke .. 2

Police: "Open the door!"
Man: "I don't want any balls!"
Police: "What? We don't have balls!"
Man: "I know."

Joke .. 3

A police officer stops a blonde for speeding and asks her very nicely if he could see her license. She replied in a huff,
'I wish you guys would get your act together. Just yesterday you took away my license and then today you expect me to show it to you!'

Joke .. 4

A woman was pulled over for speeding. This is what happened:

Woman: Is there a problem Officer.

Officer: ma'am, you were speeding.

Woman: Oh, I see.

Officer: Can I see your license please?

Woman: I'd give it to you but I don't have one.

Officer: Don't have one?

Woman: Lost it four times for drunk driving.

Officer: I see... Can I see your vehicle registration papers please.

Woman: I can't do that.

Officer: Why not?

Woman: I stole this car.

Officer: Stole it?

Woman: Yes, and I killed and hacked up the owner.

Officer: You what?

Woman: His body parts are in plastic bags in the trunk if you want to see.

The Officer looks at the woman and slowly backs away to his car and calls for back up. Within minutes 5 Police cars circle her car. A Senior Officer slowly approaches the car, clasping his half drawn gun.

Officer2: Ma'am, could you step out of the vehicle please!

The woman steps out of her vehicle.

Woman: Is there a problem sir?

Officer2: One of my Officers told me that you have stolen this car and murdered the owner.

Woman: Murdered the owner?

Officer2: Yes. Could you open the trunk of your car please.

The woman opens the trunk, revealing nothing but an empty trunk.

Officer2: Is this your car, ma'am?

Woman: Yes Officer, here are the registration papers.

The Officer is quite stunned.

Officer2: One of my Officers claims that you do not have a driver's license.

The woman digs into her handbag and pulls out a clutch purse and hands it to the Officer. The Officer snaps open the clutch purse and examines the license. He looks quite puzzled.

Officer2: Thank you ma'am. One of my Officers told me that you didn't have a license, that you stole this car and that you murdered and hacked up the owner.

Woman: Bet you the lying bastard told you I was speeding too.

FAMILY JOKES

Joke .. 1

"Daddy, what is an alcoholic?"
"Do you see those 4 trees, son? An alcoholic would see 8 trees."
"Um, Dad – there are only 2 trees."

Joke .. 2

Wife calls her mother: "Today I fought so much with my
husband. I am coming to live with you again.
Mother: No. He should pay for his mistake. I am coming to live
with you.

Joke .. 3

A boy asks his Dad one day, "Dad, why is my sister called
Paris?"
His Dad replies, "Because she was conceived in Paris."
The boy says, "Ahh, thanks Dad."
His Dad says, "You're welcome, Backseat."

Joke .. 4

Son: mom, what should I put on today?
Mother; your closet is full of good stuff.
Son: thanks mom, without your worthwhile suggestions, I
could have gone to the fridge!!

Joke .. 5

Son: dad, where is the Pacific located?
Father: I have no idea.
Son: dad, how old is the oldest turtle?
Father: I don't know.
Mother: Tom! Leave your father alone. He must be tired after a long day at work.
Father: Oh! Darling! Please let the boy ask and learn.

Joke .. 6

A boy asks his father, "Dad, are bugs good to eat?" "That's disgusting. Don't talk about things like that over dinner," the dad replies. After dinner the father asks, "Now, son, what did you want to ask me?" "Oh, nothing," the boy says. "There was a bug in your soup, but now it's gone."

Joke .. 7

A 4-year-old son was eating an apple in the back seat of the car, when he asked, "Daddy, why is my apple turning brown?"
"Because," his dad explained, "after you ate the skin off, the meat of the apple came into contact with the air, which caused it to oxidize, thus changing the molecular structure and turning it into a different color."
There was a long silence. Then the son asked softly, "Daddy, are you talking to me?"

Joke .. 8

A little girl asked her father: "How did the human race appear?"
The father answered, "God made Adam and Eve; they had children; and so was all mankind made."
Two days later the girl asked her mother the same question.
The mother answered, "Many years ago there were monkeys from which the human race evolved."
The confused girl returned to her father and said, "Dad, how is it possible that you told me the human race was created by God, and Mom said they developed from monkeys?"
The father answered, "Well, Dear, it is very simple. I told you about my side of the family, and your mother told you about hers."

Joke .. 9

Fred was saying his prayers as his father passed by his bedroom door. "God bless Mommy, and God bless Daddy, and please make Calais the capital of France."
"Fred," said his father, "why do you want Calais to be the capital of France?"
"Because that's what I wrote in my geography test!"

Joke .. 10

"Mom, teacher was asking me today if I have any brothers or sisters who will be coming to school."
"That's nice of her to take such an interest, dear. What did she say when you told her you are the only child?"
She just said, "Thank goodness!"

Joke .. 11

During a quarrel with his parents, young Michael cried,
"I want excitement, adventure, money, and beautiful women. I'll never find it here at home, so I'm leaving. Don't try and stop me!"
With that, he headed toward the door. His father rose and followed close behind. "Didn't you hear what I said?" asked Michael. "I don't want you to try and stop me!"
"Who's trying to stop you?" replied his father. "I'm going with you!"

Joke .. 12

The child comes home from his first day at school. His Mother asks,
"Well, what did you learn today?"
The kid replies, "Not enough. They want me to come back tomorrow."

Joke .. 13

Two golden agers were discussing their husbands over lunch.
"I do wish that my John would stop biting his nails.
He makes me terribly nervous."
My Fred used to do the same thing," the other woman replied.
"But I broke him of the habit."
"Really, how?" asked the first woman.
"Easy, I hid his teeth."

Joke .. 14

Three kids come to the kitchen and sit around the breakfast table. The mother asks the oldest boy what he'd like to eat.
"I'll have some fucking French toast," he says. The mother is outraged at his language, spanks him, and sends him upstairs.
She asks the middle child what he wants. "Well, I guess that leaves more fucking French toast for me," he says. She is livid, smacks him, and sends him away.
Finally she asks the youngest son what he wants for breakfast. "I don't know," he says meekly, "but I definitely don't want any fucking French toast."

TEACHERS AND
STUDENTS

Joke .. 1

A student at a management school came up to a pretty girl and hugged her without any warning.
The surprised girl said, "What was that?"
The guy smiled at her, "Direct marketing!"
The girl slapped him soundly. "What was that?!" said the boy, holding his cheek.
"Customer feedback."

Joke .. 2

"Name me five different animals, Johnny."
"The dog, the dog's brother, the dog's sister, the dog's cousin and the dog's aunt

Joke .. 3

A teacher once asked his students to put "sugar" in a sentence. A student responded "I drink hot tea after school." "So Where is the sugar?" Asked the surprised teacher. "In the tea!" Said the student.

Joke .. 4

My teachers told me I'd never amount to much because I procrastinate so much.
I told them, "Just you wait!"

Joke .. 5

What's a writing utensil's favorite place to go on vacation?
Pencil-vania!

Joke .. 6

Teacher: "Kids, what does the chicken give you?"
Student: "Meat!"
Teacher: "Very good! Now what does the pig give you?"
Student: "Bacon!"
Teacher: "Great! And what does the fat cow give you?"
Student: "Homework!"

Joke .. 7

In school canteen, there was a basket of apples with a written
note: "don't take more than 1, God is watching!"
A little further there was a box of chocolates, a naughty child
wrote:
"Take as many as you want. God is watching the apples"

Joke .. 8

A teacher asked one of the boys in her class, "Can people really
predict the future with cards?" His response is, "My mother
can." The teacher replies in disbelief, "Really?" The young boy is
quick to explain, "Yes, she takes one look at my report card and
tells me what will happen when my father gets home.

Joke .. 9

Registry on the first day back at school in Birmingham,
England.
The teacher began calling out the names of the pupils:-
"Mustafa Al Eih Zeri?" "Here"
"Ahmed El Kabul?" "Here"
"Fatima Al Hayek?" "Here"
"Ali Abdul Olmi?" "Here"

"Mohammed Bin Kadir?" "Here"
"Ali Son al En" - silence in the classroom.
"Ali Son al En" - continued silence as everyone looked around the room.
The teacher repeated the call.
A girl stood up and said, "Sorry, teacher. I think that's me. It's pronounced Alison Allen."

Joke .. 10

Once upon a time a small boy named Basheer lived in a tiny Moroccan village.
All his classmates hated him for his stupidity especially his teacher who was always yelling at him "you are driving me crazy Basheer"...
One day his mother went to check out how he is doing at school and the teacher told her honestly that her son is simply a disaster, getting very low marks and never had she seen such a dumb boy in her whole career...
The mother could not accept such a feedback and she took her son out from that school. she even shifted to another city ...
25 years later, that teacher got a cardio disorder and all the doctors have advised her to go for an open heart operation which only one surgeon could perform..
Left with no other choice she did it and the surgery was successful ...when she opened her eyes, she saw a handsome doctor smiling to her, being under anesthesia effect, she wanted to thank him but could not talk, in turn, he was staring at her face which started turning blue, she was raising her hand trying to tell him something but in vain and eventually died...
The doctor was shocked and was trying to understand what just happened, till he turned back and saw our friend
Basheer working as a cleaner in that hospital who unplugged the ventilator to connect his vacuum cleaner......
If you were thinking that Basheer became a doctor, it's because you have been watching too many Indian movies, serials or have read too many motivational forward messages off late.

HUSBAND AND WIFE

Joke .. 1

Wait for me honey, I'm just finishing my make-up.
You don't need make-up, Jane.
Oh, Richard.... really? That is so sweet of you!
You need plastic surgery.

Joke .. 2

Do you know why women aren't allowed in space?
To avoid scenarios like: "Houston, we have a problem!"
"What is the problem?"
"Yeah, great, pretend like you don't know what I'm talking about!"

Joke .. 3

Wife: Today, I want to relax,
so I have brought three movie tickets.
Husband: why three tickets?
Wife: you and your parents.

Joke .. 4

Husband sent a text to wife at night,
"Hi I will get late, plz try and wash all my dirty clothes
And make sure you prepare my favorite dish before I return."
He sent another text, "I forgot to tell u that I got an increase in
My salary at the end of month I'm getting u a new car"
She text back, "Omg really?"
Husband Replied: "No I just wanted to make sure u got my 1st msg."

Joke .. 5

A woman told her husband that she saw him with another woman in her dream. To which the man replied, 'it's only a dream'. The woman said; 'and this is what is pissing me off'!!!

Joke .. 6

Husband Sends the Following Message to His Wife
My Love,
If you're Sleeping, Send Me Your Dreams.
If you're Smiling, Send Me Your Smile.
If you're Crying, Send Me Your Tears.
I Love You.
Wife Texted Back:
I'm In the Toilet, What Should I Send You? "

Joke .. 7

A husband and wife were having dinner at a very fine restaurant when this absolutely stunning young woman comes over to their table, gives the husband a big kiss, tells him she'll see him later, and walks away.
His wife glares at him and says, "Who was that??!!"
"Oh," replies the husband, "that was my mistress."
The wife says, "That's it; I want a divorce."
"I understand," replies her husband, "but, remember, if you get a divorce, there will be no more shopping trips to Paris, no wintering in the Caribbean, no Lexus in the garage, and no more country club. But the decision is yours."
Just then the wife notices a mutual friend entering the restaurant with a gorgeous woman.
"Who's that woman with Jim?" she asks.
"That's his mistress," replies her husband.
"Ours is prettier," says the wife.

Joke .. 8

The poor country pastor was livid when he confronted his wife with the receipt for a $250 dress she had bought.
"How could you do this!" he exclaimed.
"I don't know," she wailed, "I was standing in the store looking at the dress. Then I found myself trying it on. It was like the Devil was whispering to me, 'Gee, you look great in that dress. You should buy it.'"

"Well," the pastor persisted, "You know how to deal with him! Just tell him, "Get behind me, Satan!"
"I did," replied his wife, "but then he said 'It looks great from back here, too!'"

Joke .. 9

A wife sends her programmer husband for grocery shopping.
She tells him: I need butter, sugar and cooking oil. Also, get a loaf of bread and if they have eggs, get 6.
The husband returns with the butter, sugar and cooking oil, as well as 6 loaves of bread.
The wife asks: Why the hell did you get 6 loaves of bread?
To which the husband replies: They had eggs.

Joke .. 10

A woman with 14 children, ranging in age from one to fourteen, went to court to sue her husband for divorce on grounds of desertion.
"When did he leave you?" the judge asked.
"Thirteen years ago," the tired mother replied.
The judge was confused, "Well, if he left thirteen years ago, where did all these children come from?"
"Well," said the woman, "he kept coming back to say he was sorry."

Joke .. 11

A man said to his wife one day, "I don't know how you can be so stupid and so beautiful all at the same time.
"The wife responded, "Allow me to explain. God made me beautiful so you would be attracted to me; God made me stupid so I would be attracted to you!

Joke .. 12

A couple drove down a country road for several miles, not saying a word. An earlier discussion had led to an argument and neither of them wanted to concede their position. As they passed a barnyard of mules, goats, and pigs, the husband asked sarcastically, "Relatives of yours?" "Yep," the wife replied , "in-laws

Joke .. 13

A man and his wife were having some problems at home and were giving each other the silent treatment. Suddenly, the man realized that the next day, he would need his wife to wake him at 5:00 AM for an early morning business flight. Not wanting to be the first to break the silence (and LOSE), he wrote on a piece of paper,
"Please wake me at 5:00 AM " He left it where he knew she would find it. The next morning, the man woke up, only to discover it was 9:00 AM and he had missed his flight. Furious, he was about to go and see why his wife hadn't wakened him, when he noticed a piece of paper by the bed. The paper said,
"It is 5:00 AM. Wake up." Men are not equipped for these kinds of contests.

Joke .. 14

Question: If your dog is barking at the back door and your wife is yelling at the front door, who do you let in first?
Answer; The dog, of course. He'll shut up once you let him in.

Joke .. 15

Wife: 'What are you doing?'
Husband: Nothing.
Wife: 'Nothing...? You've been reading our marriage certificate for an hour.'

Husband: 'I was looking for the expiration date.'

Joke .. 16

One spelling mistake in hurry can make hell!
Husband wrote a romantic message to his wife on his official trip and missed an "e" in the last word.
Now he is seeking police protection to enter his own house....
He wrote "Hi darling I'm experiencing the best time of my life & I wish you were her!!"
Game over!

Joke .. 17

A man received a letter from some kidnappers. The letter said, "If you don't promise to send us $100,000, we promise you we will kidnap your wife."
The poor man wrote back,
" I am afraid I can't keep my promise but I hope you will keep yours."

Joke .. 18

Two men are having a conversation.
"I would like to see a woman dentist," said the first man.
"Why?" asked his friend?
"Because it would be a pleasure to have a woman say, 'open your mouth' instead of 'shut up.'"

Joke .. 19

Honey," said a husband to his wife, "I've invited a friend home for supper."
"What? Are you crazy? The house is a mess, I didn't go shopping, all the dishes are dirty, and I don't feel like cooking a fancy meal!"
"I know all that." "Then why did you invite a friend for supper?"
"Because the poor fool's thinking about getting married."

Joke .. 20

An airline introduced a special package for businessmen. Buy your ticket; get your wife's ticket free.
After a great success, the airline sent letters to all the wives asking how the trip was. All of them gave the same reply, "Which trip?"

Joke .. 21

A lady says to her doctor: "My husband has a habit of talking in his sleep! What should I give him to cure it?"
The doctor replies: "Give him the opportunity to speak while he's awake!"

Joke .. 22

The wife was screaming at her Husband:
"Leave!! Get out of this house!" she ordered.
As he was walking out the door she yelled,
"And ... I hope you die a slow and painful death!"
He turned around and replied
"So now you want me to stay?"

OLD PEOPLE

Joke .. 1

A pilot forgot the mike on as he said to himself; 'I'm gonna have lunch and then kiss the attendant. As the flight attended and the passengers heard that, the flight battement rushed to turn the mike off and while running she stumbled on an old woman's foot. The old woman said angrily: ' What's the rush!!!! Don't you understand!! He said he would have lunch first'.

Joke .. 2

One day, Gramma sent her grandson Little Johnny down to the water hole to get some water for cooking dinner. As he was dipping the bucket in, he saw two big eyes looking back at him. He dropped the bucket and hightailed it for Gramma's kitchen.
"Well now, where's my bucket and where's my water?" Gramma asked him.
"I can't get any water from that water hole, Gramma!" exclaimed Little Johnny. "There's a big ol' alligator down there waiting for me!"
"Now don't you mind that ol' alligator, Little Johnny. He's been there for a few years now, and he's never hurt anyone. Why, he's probably as scared of you as you are of him!"
"Well, Gramma," replied Little Johnny, "if he's as scared of me as I am of him, then that water ain't fit to drink!"

Joke .. 3

Two elderly gentlemen from a retirement center were sitting on a bench under a tree when one turns to the other and says: 'Slim, I'm 83 years old now and I'm just full of aches and pains. I know you're about my age. How do you feel?'
Slim says, 'I feel just like a newborn baby.' 'Really!? Like a newborn baby!?' Yep. No hair, no teeth, and I think I just wet my pants.'

Joke .. 4

An elderly couple were driving across the country. The woman was driving when she got pulled over by the highway patrol. The officer said, "Ma'am did you know you were speeding?"
The woman turns to her husband and asked, "What did he say?"
The old man yelled, "He says you were speeding!"
The patrolman said, "May I see your license?"
The woman turned to her husband and asked, "What did he say?"
The old man yelled, "He wants to see your license!"
The woman gave him her license. The patrolman said, "I see you are from Texas. I spent some time there once and went on a blind date with the ugliest woman I've ever seen."
The woman turned to her husband and asked, "What did he say?" The old man yelled, "He thinks he knows you!"

Joke .. 5

An older couple were lying in bed one night. The husband was falling asleep but the wife was in a romantic mood and wanted to talk.

She said, "You used to hold my hand when we were courting." Wearily he reached across, held her hand for a second and tried to get back to sleep. A few moments later she said,

"Then you used to kiss me." Mildly irritated, he reached across, gave her a peck on the cheek and settled down to sleep. Thirty seconds later she said,

"Then you used to bite my neck." Angrily, he threw back the bed clothes and got out of bed. "Where are you going?" she asked.

"To get my teeth!"

Joke .. 6

A man visits his aunt in the nursing home. It turns out that she is taking a nap, so he just sits down in a chair in her room, flips through a few magazines, and munches on some peanuts sitting in a bowl on the table. Eventually, the aunt wakes up, and her nephew realizes he's absentmindedly finished the entire bowl.

"I'm so sorry, auntie, I've eaten all of your peanuts!"

"That's okay, dearie," the aunt replied.

"After I've sucked the chocolate off, I don't care for them anyway."

Joke .. 7

The elderly husband and wife, both a little hard of hearing, were watching golf on TV. The husband turned to his wife of some 50 years and said,

"In my next life, I'm going to be rich and play all those beautiful golf courses with their great bars and dining and dancing areas."

The wife quickly responded, "How will you be able to manage all that with your bad legs? You can barely walk!"
"I said, '...in my next life...,'" the husband replied.
"Oh," she said. "I thought you said, 'With my next wife!'"

Joke .. 8

Two old women were sitting on a bench waiting for their bus.
The buses were running late, and a lot of time passed.
Finally, one woman turned to the other and said,
"You know, I've been sitting here so long, my butt fell asleep!"
The other woman turned to her and said, "I know! I heard it snoring!"

Joke .. 9

Shortly after an International Airways flight had reached its cruising altitude, the captain announced: 'Ladies and Gentlemen, this is your Captain. Welcome to Flight 293, non-stop from *** to ***. The weather ahead is good, so we should have a smooth uneventful flight. So sit back, relax and... OH, MY GOD!'
Silence followed!
Some moments later the captain came back on the intercom.
'Ladies and gentlemen, I'm sorry if I scared you. While I was talking to you, a flight attendant accidentally spilled a cup of hot coffee in my lap. You should see the front of my pants!'
An elderly passenger yelled back... 'For Christ sake... You should see the back of mine!'

ANIMALS

Joke .. 1

What is black – white – black – white – black – white? A penguin rolling down a mountain!

Joke .. 2

How many tickles does it take to get an octopus to laugh?
Ten tickles.

Joke .. 3

A Baldy man observes something crawling over his head, as he puts his hand on it, he finds out that it is an ant. That ant looks at him and says; 'please, sir; just let me back for one more minute, I'd like to have the last slide!!!

Joke .. 4

A drunk man holding a bat, looking at it and laughing loud nonstop. People asked him why he was laughing. He said that this was the first time he saw a Mouse in disguise.

Joke .. 5

A man riding out in the bush fell from his horse and broke his leg. He was a long way out, so the situation looked pretty grim. Then the horse grabbed the man's belt in his teeth and dragged him to the shade of a nearby tree. He made the man as comfortable as he could and then galloped off to get help. The man discussed the incident a few weeks later with a friend. The friend was very, very, impressed and praised the horse's intelligence. "He's not so smart," said the animal's owner. "He came back with a vet."

Joke .. 6

A DEA officer stopped at a farm one day " I need to inspect your farm for illegal growing drugs."

The farmer replies, pointing with his fingers " Okay,But dont go into the field over there....."
The DEA officer verbally explodes saying "Mister, I have the authority of the Federal Government with me!"
Reaching into his rear pant's pocket, the arrogant officer removed his badge and shoved it in the farmers face. " See this fucking badge?! This badge means that I am allowed to go anywhere I wish.....on any land!! No questions asked or answers given!! Have I made myself clear?.....Do you understand?"
The guy nods politely, apologizes and goes about his chores. A short while later, he hears loud screams. He looks up and sees the DEA officer running for his life, being chased by the guy's big old mean bull..... With every step the bull was gaining ground on the officer and it seemed likely that he would surely be gored before he reached safety. The officer was clearly terrified.
The guy throws down his tools, runs to the fence and yells at the top of his voice.....
"Your badge, show him your fucking BADGE!!!!......"

Joke .. 7

Once upon a time there was a shepherd looking after his sheep on the side of a deserted road. Suddenly a brand new Porsche, screeches to a halt. The driver, a man dressed in Armani suit, Cerruti shoes, Ray Ban sunglasses, Tag her wrist watch and Pierre Cardin tie gets out and asks the Shepherd," If I can tell you how many sheep you have, will you give me one of them?"
The shepherd looks at the young man then looks at the large flock of grazing sheep and replies "Okay".

The young man parks the car, connects his laptop to the mobile-fax, enters a NASA website, scans the ground using his GPS,opens a database & 60 excel tables filled with algorithm & pivot tables. He then prints out a 150 page report on his high-tech mini printer, turns to the shepherd and says," You have exactly 1586 sheep". The shepherd cheers, " That's correct, you can have your sheep".

The young man takes one of the animal from the flock and puts it in the back of his Porsche.

The shepherd looks at him and asks," If I guess your profession, will you return my animal to me?"

The young man answers," Yes, why not?"

The shepherd says, " You are an Consultant"

"How did you know?" asks the young man.

"Very simple" answers the shepherd. " Firstly, you came here without being wanted. Secondly, you charged me a fee, to tell me something I already know. Thirdly, you don't understand anything about my business.... Now can I have my DOG back!

Joke .. 8

A turtle was walking down an alley in New York when he was mugged by a gang of snails. A police detective came to investigate and asked the turtle if he could explain what happened.

The turtle looked at the detective with a confused look on his face and replied "I don't know, it all happened so fast."

Joke .. 9

An Alsatian went to a telegram office, took out a blank form and wrote, "Woof. Woof. Woof. Woof. Woof. Woof. Woof. Woof. Woof."

The clerk examined the paper and politely told the dog: "There are only nine words here. You could send another 'Woof' for the same price."

"But," the dog replied, "that would make no sense at all

STUPID PEOPLE

Joke .. 1

It is evening. Little Johnny and his friend are sitting by a camp fire. They've been plagued by swarms of mosquitoes already for an hour and the assault only worsens when the darkness sets in. Suddenly, fireflies appear. Little Johnny swears: "These darn mosquitoes! Now they've even brought lanterns with them to find us!"

Joke .. 2

A man whose phone was stolen has just been to the police station. Upon hearing his complaint; the police assured him that they will bring his phone back even if it was hidden underground. As he was coming back home, he saw some men digging down the street. He stopped and said: "Mind you guys; my phone is black."

Joke .. 3

A drunk man came to a supermarket and asked them to give him a pack of cigarettes. The sales assistant told him that they ran out.
 The man entered another shop and said to the workers over there. "Hey guys! How about you? Don't say you don't have too"
..

Joke .. 4

A Russian, an American, and a Blonde were talking one day. The Russian said, 'We were the first in space!' The American said, 'We were the first on the moon!' The Blonde said, 'So what? We're going to be the first on the sun!' The Russian and the American looked at each other and shook their heads. 'You can't land on the sun, you idiot! You'll burn up!' said the Russian. To which the Blonde replied, 'We're not stupid, you know We're going at night!'

Joke .. 5

A bank robber pulls out gun points it at the teller, and says, "Give me all the money or you're geography!" The puzzled teller replies, "Did you mean to say 'or you're history?'" The robber says, "Don't change the subject!"

Joke .. 6

A man went to prison and heard an inmate say, "274". Then everybody laughed. The man asked him what was so funny? He said, "We've been here so long, that we numbered all the jokes, cause we've heard 'em all." The man thinks for a second, and randomly says, "4,357." Everyone gets silent, and then all of a sudden, thunderous laughter. The inmate says, "We've never heard that one before."

Joke .. 7

A bloke walks into a Glasgow library and says to the prim librarian, 'Excuse me Miss, dey ye hiv ony books on suicide?' To which she stops doing her tasks, looks at him over the top of her glasses and says, 'Fook off, ye'll no bring it back!'

Joke .. 8

Two men were walking home after a Halloween party and decided to take a shortcut through the cemetery just for laughs. Right in the middle of the cemetery, they were startled by a tap-tap-tapping noise coming from the misty shadows.
Trembling with fear, they found an old man with a hammer and chisel, chipping away at one of the headstones.
"Holy cow, Mister," one of them said after catching his breath. "You scared us half to death - we thought you were a ghost! What are you doing working here so late at night?"
"Those fools!" the old man grumbled. "They misspelled my name!"

Joke .. 9

One day, a mailman was greeted by a boy and his dog.
The mailman said to the boy, "Does your dog bite?"
"No," replied the boy. Just then, the dog bit the mailman.
"Hey, "he yelled. "I thought your dog doesn't bite!"
"He doesn't," replied the boy, "but that's not my dog."

Joke .. 10

Sardar to Librarian: l want a book named "Psycho The Rapist".
The Librarian searched for 3 hrs then came back & Slapped the
Sardar & said Idiot the book name is "Psychotherapist"

Joke .. 11

A Cub Scout troop was half an hour late to its den meeting. The
den mother asked them severely, "Why are you so late?" "Oh,"
said one boy, "we were helping an old man cross the street."
"That's a nice thing for scouts to do," said the mother. She
paused. "But it shouldn't make you half an hour late." "Well,
you see," said another boy, "he didn't want to go."

Joke .. 12

A blonde husband spoke frantically into the phone: "My wife is
pregnant and her contractions are only two minutes apart!" "Is
this her first child?" the emergency operator asked. "No, you
idiot!" the blonde shouted. "This is her husband!"

Joke .. 13

A young man was walking past an old woman on a street
corner, when she said, "Son, if it is not too much trouble, can
you see me across the street." The young man said, "Just a
minute." Then he walked across the street, looked back and
yelled, "Yes, I can see you!"

Joke .. 14

A woman saw an ad in the local newspaper which read: "Purebred Police Dog $25. Free local delivery." Thinking that to be a great bargain, she called and ordered the dog to be delivered. The next day a van arrived at her home and delivered the mangiest-looking mongrel she had ever seen! In a rage, she telephoned the man who had placed the ad, "How dare you call that mangy mutt a pure bred police dog!?" "Don't let his looks deceive you, ma'am," the man replied. "He's in the Secret Service."

Joke .. 15

The other day I needed to pay a visit to the public toilet, so I found a public toilet that had two cubicles.
One of the doors was locked. So I went into the other one, closed the door, dropped my trousers and sat down.
A voice came from the cubicle next to me: "Hello mate, how are you doing?"
Although I thought that it was a bit strange, I didn't want to be rude, so I replied, "Not too bad, thanks."
After a short pause, I heard the voice again. "So, what are you up to?"
Again I answered, somewhat reluctantly, "Just having a quick shit... How about yourself?"
The next thing I heard him say was, "Sorry, mate, I'll have to call you back. I've got some cunt in the cubicle next to me answering everything I say."

Joke .. 16

One day a big group of blondes met in New York city to show the world that blondes aren't dumb. They said:
"Ask us any qn, & we'll show you that we aren't dumb."
The group caught the attention of a passer-by, who agreed to ask them some qns.

He randomly picked a blonde from the crowd & asked: "What is the 1st month of the year?" "November?", answered the blonde. "Nope", said the man. Now the crowd began to chant, "Give her another chance." So the man asked: "What's the capital of U.S.A.?" The blonde responded: "Paris?" "Wrong again", said the man. Again the crowd chanted: "Give her another chance." Man: "Okay, but this is the last one. What's one plus one?" The blonde replied: "Two?" "Give her another chance; "Give her another chance.", screamed the crowd.

Joke .. 17

One afternoon a wealthy manager was driving in his limousine when he saw two men along the roadside eating grass.
Disturbed by the sight, he ordered his driver to stop and he got out to investigate. He asked one man "Why are you eating grass?"
"We don't have any money for food," the poor man replied. "We have to eat grass."
"Well, then, you can come with me to my house and I'll feed you" the manager said.
"But sir, I have a wife and two children with me. They are over there, under that tree".
"Bring them along," the manager replied. Turning to the other poor man he stated, "You come with us also."
The second man, in a pitiful voice then said, "But sir, I also have a wife and six children with me!"
"Bring them all, as well," the manager answered.
They all entered the car, which was no easy task, even for a car as large as the limousine was.
Once underway, one of the poor fellows turned to mr. Manager and said, "Sir, you are too kind. Thank you for taking all of us with you."
The manager replied, "Glad to do it. You'll really love my place; the grass is almost 1 meter high!"

MISCELLANEUOS

Joke .. 1

Harry prays to God: Dear Lord, please make me win the lottery.
The next day Harry begs the Lord again: Please make it so I win the lottery, Lord!
The next day, Harry again prays: Please, please, dear Lord, make me win the lottery!
Suddenly he hears a voice from above: Harry, would you kindly go and buy a lottery ticket.

Joke .. 2

Three tomatoes are walking down the street. Papa Tomato, Mama Tomato and Baby Tomato. Baby Tomato starts lagging behind, and Papa Tomato gets really angry. Goes back and squishes him and says: "Ketchup".

Joke .. 3

As soon as the thief broke into a house, he was caught by an overweight woman who knocked him down and sat above him. "Hey, Johnny! Hurry up and inform your daddy I caught a thief." The woman called. The desperate thief shouted as he was stifling ... "Ppppppplease,,, hurrrrrry up, Joooohhhhhnnyyyy."

Joke .. 4

A young brave visits the chief of the tribe with a question. "Wise one, is it true you name all the members of the tribe, and if so, how is it done?"

The venerable old man replies "Yes, for over 20 years I have named each person who is born to the tribe. I sit outside the lodge, and when I hear the infants' first cry, I open my eyes and the first thing I see becomes the name. So it was with your brother Big Bear, your sister Singing Bird, your cousin Blue Cloud, and so on."

"But tell me, Two Dogs F------ why do you ask?"

Joke .. 5

Christopher: Hey dad, you wanna hear something funny? There was a man who was drowning, and a boat came, and the man on the boat said "Do you need help?" and the man said "God will save me". Then another boat came and he tried to help him, but he said "God will save me", then he drowned and went to Heaven. Then the man told God, "God, why didn't you save me?" and God said "I sent you two boats, you dummy!"

Joke .. 6

Two cannibals were eating a clown. One turns to the other and says: "Does this taste funny to you?"

Joke .. 7

An excited girl once posted on Facebook after getting lots of likes and comments; 'I feell I'm gona take over the whol werld one daı'.
One of the comments went 'dear friend, take control over your keyboard first of all; and then we can give the world a second thought!!'

Joke .. 8

When some of those enthusiastic guys, who hasn't played football for ages, comes back from a football match over the weekend and starts relating his heroic acts and plays, you would think that the match was a World Cup final. But as you take a look at him running, an image of an ostrich running in a documentary dates back to the 1900s will come to your mind.

Joke .. 9

What did the nose say to the finger?
Quit picking on me.

Joke .. 10

What did the left eye say to the right eye?
Between you and me, something smells.

Joke .. 11

The phrase 'shut up' is acceptable in one case only. When you ask to pay after doing the shopping and the assistant tells you to shut up.

Joke .. 12

A nice, calm and respectable lady went into the pharmacy, right up to the pharmacist, looked straight into his eyes, and said, "I would like to buy some cyanide."

The pharmacist asked, "Why in the world do you need cyanide?"

The lady replied, "I need it to poison my husband."

The pharmacists eyes got big and he exclaimed, "Lord have mercy! I can't give you cyanide to kill your husband! That's against the law! I'll lose my license! They'll throw both of us in jail! All kinds of bad things will happen. Absolutely not! You CANNOT have any cyanide!"

The lady reached into her purse and pulled out a picture of her husband in bed with the pharmacist's wife.

The pharmacist looked at the picture and replied, "Well now. That's different. You didn't tell me you had a prescription."

Joke .. 13

A boss announces to his staff: "I've lost a wallet with 500 dollars, if you find it, I'm offering a 100 dollars finder's fee!" A voice in the background says: "I'm offering 200.

Joke .. 14

A motorist, driving by a Texas ranch, hit and killed a calf that was crossing the road. The driver went to the owner of the calf and explained what had happened. He then asked what the animal was worth.

"Oh, about $200 today," said the rancher. "But in six years it would have been worth $900. So $900 is what I'm out."

The motorist sat down and wrote out a check and handed it to the farmer.

"Here is the check for $900. It's postdated six years from now

Joke .. 15

A judge working a double-homicide case tells the defendant,
 "You're charged with beating your wife to death with a hammer."

"You bastard!" yells a voice from the back of the courtroom.

 "You're also charged with killing your mother-in-law with a hammer," says the judge.

 "Bastard!" the same person yells. The judge addresses the man sitting in the back of the courtroom. "Sir, one more outburst and I'll charge you with contempt."

"I'm sorry, Your Honor," says the man. "But I've been this bastard's neighbor for 10 years, and every time I asked to borrow a hammer, he said he didn't have one."

Joke .. 16

Death came to a guy and said, "My friend, today is your day"!
Guy:- "But I'm not ready!".
Then death said, "Well your name is the next on my list..."
Guy:- "Okay why don't you take a seat and I will get you something to eat before we go?".
Then death said, "All right.. ".
The guy gave death some food with sleeping pills in it, death finished eating and fell into a deep sleep.
The guy took the list & removed his name from top of the list and put into the bottom of the list.
When death woke up he said to the guy:
"Because you have been so very nice to me, I will start from the BOTTOM of the list.."

Joke .. 17

At a girl's college dormitory, dates were permitted only on Saturday night. One young man showed up on a Tuesday evening, explaining to an older woman in the lobby of the dorm that it was imperative he see a certain young lady immediately. "I want to surprise her. You see, I'm her brother." "Oh, she'll be surprised all right," said the woman. "But think of how surprised I am! I'm her mother!"

Joke .. 18

Joe was a flight attendant for an airline. He watched as an older lady boarded the plane holding a dog in a cage. "Excuse me," said Joe, "Dogs are not allowed on board; you have to check it in with the baggage." The lady wasn't happy, but Joe succeeded in convincing the lady without much of a scene. Upon arrival, Joe took a peek in the cage, and to his great surprise, saw that the dog was dead! Frantic that they may get sued, Joe quickly sent one of his underlings out to town to buy a dog that looked exactly the same. Just in the nick of time the underling arrived with the dog. They quickly switched dogs and breathed a sigh of relief. "This isn't my dog!" said the lady as soon as she saw it. "I'm sure it is" insisted Joe "I was very careful about where I put it." "It's not my dog" argued the lady, "you see, I was bringing my dog to my home town to have him buried, and this dog is alive!"

Joke .. 19

A young lady visited a computer dating service and requested, "I'm looking for a spouse. Can you please help me to find a suitable one?"
The matchmaker said, "What exactly are you looking for?"
"Well, let me see. Needs to be good looking, polite, humorous, sporty, knowledgeable, good at singing and dancing. Willing to accompany me the whole day at home during my leisure hour if I don't go out.
Be able to tell me interesting stories when I need a companion for conversation and be silent when I want to rest." 61
The matchmaker entered the information into the computer and, in a matter of moments, handed the result to the woman.
The result read,
"Buy a television."

Joke .. 20

A man was taking it easy, laying on the grass and looking up at the clouds. He was identifying shapes when he decided to talk to God. "God", he said, "how long is a million years?" God answered, "In my frame of reference, it's about a minute." The man asked, "God, how much is a million dollars?" God answered, "To me, it's a penny." The man then asked, "God, can I have a penny?" God answered, "In a minute."

Joke .. 21

A man lost both ears in an accident. No plastic surgeon could offer him a solution. He heard of a very good one in Sweden, and went to him. The new surgeon examined him, thought a while, and said, "Yes, I can put you right." After the operation, bandages off, stitches out, he goes to his hotel. The morning after, in a rage, he calls his surgeon, and yells, "You swine, you gave me a woman's ears." "Well, an ear is an ear; it makes no difference whether it is a man's or a woman's." "You're wrong, I hear everything, but I don't understand a thing!

Joke .. 22

Boss hangs a notice in office:
"I'm the boss. Don't forget!"
When he returns from lunch, someone wrote under it:
"Your wife called up, she wants her notice back at home."

Joke .. 23

An Englishman, a Canadian and an American were captured by terrorists.

The terrorist leader said, "Before we shoot you, you will be allowed last words. Please let me know what you wish to talk about." The Englishman replied, "I wish to speak of loyalty and service to the crown." The Canadian replied, "Since you are involved in a question of national purpose, national identity, and secession, I wish to talk about the history of constitutional process in Canada, special status, distinct society and uniqueness within diversity."

The American replied, "Just shoot me before the Canadian starts talking.

Joke .. 24

Three engineers and three lawyers are taking a trip together via train. The lawyers buy one ticket per person, but the engineers only buy one total.

"How are you going to get away with that?" the lawyers ask.

"Watch and learn," say the engineers.

So they all board the train, and when the conductor begins collecting tickets, the three engineers cram themselves into a bathroom. The conductor knocks on the door and says, "Ticket, please." A single hand sticks out and gives him the ticket. In this way, all three engineers manage to ride the train on one ticket.

The lawyers are clearly impressed. On the return trip, they only buy one ticket for all three of them. The engineers, however, don't buy any at all.

"How are you going to get away with that?" the lawyers ask.

"Watch and learn," say the engineers.

On the train home, the lawyers cram themselves into one of the bathrooms. An engineer walks over, knocks on the door, and says, "Ticket, please."

Joke .. 25

One young man went for an IAS Interview.

"When did India get independence? " He was asked.

"The efforts began a few years earlier and final result was in 1947" He replied.

"Who was responsible for our independence? "

"There were so many. Whom to mention? If I name one, it will be a injustice to another. " He replied.

"Is corruption the number one enemy in our country?"

"Some research is going on the subject and I can answer with certainly only after seeing the report" He replied.

The interview board was very pleased with his original and thoughtful answers and asked him not to reveal the questions to others, since they were planning to ask the same questions.

When he went out naturally others were curious to know what was asked. He politely declined, but one persistent Santa would not leave him. "At least tell me the answers" he pleaded, and our friend obliged.

Then it was the turn of this Santa. When he went inside, since his resume was slightly illegible, the board member asked him." By the way, what is your date of birth?"

He replied, " The effort began a few years earlier and final result was in 1947."

Somewhat puzzled, they asked another clarification. "What is your fathers' name?"

He replied, "There were so many. Whom to mention". If I name onc, it will be injustice to another".

The interviewer was incensed.

" Hey! Are you mad or what?"

He replied. "Some research is going on the subject. I can answer with certainty only after seeing the report. "

Joke .. 26

Customer: What would you recommend from the menu?

Waitress: The beef tongue is very good today.

Customer: Yeech! I'd never eat anything that came from an animal's mouth.

Waitress: Okay. How about some eggs?

Joke .. 27

A guy goes into a bank.

The clerk says,'Can I help you, sir'

He goes, ' Yea ass I wanna open an account'

Clerk, 'Please there's no need for cursing' 'Sir I'll help you but watch your language'

So the manager comes over,' Is there a problem here?'

Dude says,' I'm trying to open an account and this ass won't let me.'

'Please sir don't curse and how much are you opening the account with?'

Dude,' 7 million $'

Manager,' And this ass ain't helping' you?'

Joke .. 28

The CIA decides that it's time to begin taking out all of the terrorists and decides to hire a professional assassin. They narrow a huge field of candidates down to two men and one woman.

They bring the first guy into a room with these big steel doors at one end, slap a revolver in his hand and tell him, "Behind those doors is your wife sitting in a chair. Go in and kill her."

The guy recoils in horror and exclaims, "I can't kill my wife!"

They grab the gun away and kick him out. Then they bring in the next guy, slap the revolver in his hand and point him towards the steel doors saying, "Behind those doors is your wife sitting in a chair. Go in and kill her."

The guy goes in. The steel doors slam. Then after three minutes of silence, he comes out sobbing in tears and says, "I just can't kill my wife."

They immediately grab the gun away and throw him out as well. Next, they bring in the woman, place the gun in her hand and tell her, "Behind those doors is your husband sitting in a chair. Go in and kill him."

She goes in. The doors slam. You hear six shots in rapid succession and then, suddenly, there's all this yelling, screaming and thudding about.

Finally, the steel doors open and out walks the woman carrying the gun and wiping her brow. She tells the CIA guys, "This gun was full of blanks. I had to beat him to death with the chair!"

Other Works By the Teacher

Other works by the author

Phrasal Verbs (Advanced) The Comprehensive Collection: 1060 Common Phrasal Verbs with Plenty of Examples & Synonyms
https://www.amazon.com/dp/B09NGYYCH8

ADVANCED ENGLISH: Idioms, Phrasal Verbs, Vocabulary and Phrases: 700 Expressions of Academic Language
https://www.amazon.com/dp/B07RTGWH5X

Advanced English Collocations & Phrases in Dialogues: Master English Collocations with the Aid of Functional Dialogues once and for all https://www.amazon.com/dp/B086JYB24J

Advanced English Collocations & Phrases in Dialogues (2)
https://www.amazon.com/dp/B0B752S8S4

Advanced English Conversations (1): Speak English Like a Native
https://www.amazon.com/dp/B09PLD4GHN

Advanced English Conversations (2): Speak English Like a Native
https://www.amazon.com/dp/B089YTQPTV

Advanced English Conversations (3); Speak English Like a Native
https://www.amazon.com/dp/B0B2SD8TNF

Advanced English Conversation in Dialogues
https://www.amazon.com/dp/B0BBL1HB24

American Idioms and Idiomatic Phrases In Use (1)
https://www.amazon.com/dp/B0BH2W3MB9

TOEFL VOCABULARY (Adjectives)
https://www.amazon.com/dp/B0BD9FR6X2

TOEFL VOCABULARY (NOUNS)
https://www.amazon.com/dp/B0BK9S22RF

Daily English Expressions: Speak English Like a Native
https://www.amazon.com/dp/B0BLHXZJL8

Daily English Expressions (book - 2): Speak English Like a Native
https://www.amazon.com/dp/B0BMYRBJZF

Daily English Expressions (book - 3): Speak English Like a Native
https://www.amazon.com/dp/B0BNGPCVNQ

Daily English Expressions (Book - 4) : Speak English Like a Native
https://www.amazon.com/dp/B0BP5CPPNX

Daily English Expressions (Book - 5) : Speak English Like a Native
https://www.amazon.com/dp/B0BQFMGN6J

Daily English Expressions (Book - 6): Speak English Like a Native
https://www.amazon.com/dp/B0BRWLGYT9

Daily English Expressions (Book - 7): Speak English Like a Native
https://www.amazon.com/dp/B0BSR71WZH

Daily English Expressions (Book - 8): Speak English Like a Native
https://www.amazon.com/dp/B0BTMLFVCN

Daily English Expressions (Book - 9): Speak English Like a Native
https://www.amazon.com/dp/B0BVP8F7N1

Daily English Expressions (Book - 10): Speak English Like a Native
https://www.amazon.com/dp/B0BXBC5L52

Spoken English Phrases (book - 2): Speak English Like a Native

https://www.amazon.com/dp/B0C18X5T1Y

Spoken English Phrases (book - 1): Speak English Like a Native

https://www.amazon.com/dp/B0C18Z2X52

End of the Book

www.ingramcontent.com/pod-product-compliance
Lightning Source LLC
Chambersburg PA
CBHW051400280526
45784CB00007B/3043